Marketing Mavericks:

Unlocking Success with Modern Warfare Strategies

Part-1 (General Strategies)

Part-2 (Digital Strategies)

Part-1

Introduction

In today's fiercely competitive business landscape, companies constantly strive for an edge over their rivals. The concept of "marketing warfare" offers a strategic framework for achieving dominance in the marketplace. This book delves into powerful marketing warfare techniques, each accompanied by detailed case studies illustrating their application and impact. Through meticulous analysis and real-world examples, readers will gain invaluable insights into how these techniques can be leveraged to outmanoeuvre competitors and secure market leadership.

Throughout the following chapters, we'll explore various tactics ranging from offensive manoeuvres aimed at seizing market share to defensive strategies designed to protect against competitive threats. Drawing on the wisdom of renowned marketing strategists and successful companies, this book provides a comprehensive guide to navigating the battleground of modern business.

Let's embark on a journey through the realms of marketing warfare, where cunning strategies and bold actions determine the victors in the battle for consumer attention and loyalty.

Chapter 1
Offensive Marketing Strategies

Market Segmentation

Market segmentation is a multifaceted approach that involves dividing a broad market into smaller, more manageable segments based on various criteria such as demographics, psychographics, geographic location, and behavioural patterns. This strategic manoeuvre enables companies to better understand and cater to the diverse needs and preferences of distinct consumer groups.

Understanding Consumer Needs:

Effective market segmentation begins with a deep understanding of consumer needs, desires, and buying behaviours. By conducting thorough market research and analysis, businesses can identify commonalities and differences among various consumer segments. This insight allows them to develop tailored marketing strategies and product offerings that resonate with specific target audiences.

Targeting Specific Segments:

Once different segments are identified, businesses can prioritize their resources and efforts towards segments that offer the greatest potential for profitability and growth. By targeting specific segments with customized marketing messages and product offerings, companies can enhance their relevance and appeal to consumers, ultimately driving higher sales and market share.

Example Case Study: Coca-Cola vs. Pepsi

A classic example of effective market segmentation can be seen in the long-standing rivalry between Coca-Cola and Pepsi. Both companies target multiple consumer segments but employ different strategies to appeal to them.

Coca-Cola has historically focused on creating a universal appeal with its timeless brand image and messaging. However, the company also recognizes the importance of catering to diverse consumer preferences. For example, it introduced Diet Coke to target health-conscious consumers and Coke Zero for those seeking a zero-calorie option.

On the other hand, Pepsi has adopted a more youth-oriented approach, positioning itself as the choice of the younger generation with its bold marketing campaigns and partnerships with celebrities and pop culture icons. Additionally, Pepsi has diversified its product portfolio to include variations like Pepsi Max and Pepsi Lime to appeal to specific taste preferences within different segments.

Conclusion:

Market segmentation is a vital component of offensive marketing strategies, enabling companies to identify and capitalize on opportunities for growth and expansion. By understanding the unique needs and preferences of distinct consumer segments, businesses can tailor their marketing efforts and product offerings to maximize relevance and appeal, ultimately gaining a competitive edge in the marketplace.

Chapter 2
Positioning Strategies

Differentiation

Differentiation is a crucial aspect of positioning strategies, allowing companies to distinguish their products or services from those of competitors in the minds of consumers. By highlighting unique features, benefits, or attributes, businesses can create a perception of superiority and value, thereby influencing purchasing decisions.

Creating Unique Value Propositions:

Effective differentiation begins with identifying and communicating a compelling value proposition that sets a brand apart from its competitors. This involves understanding the needs and preferences of target customers and developing offerings that address those needs in a distinct and meaningful way. Whether through product innovation, superior quality, exceptional service, or brand image, differentiation creates a competitive advantage that attracts and retains customers.

Example Case Study: Apple Inc.

Apple Inc. is renowned for its masterful use of differentiation in positioning its products within the highly competitive technology industry. From the sleek design of its hardware to the intuitive user interface of its software, Apple creates products that stand out in terms of both form and function.

One of Apple's most notable differentiators is its ecosystem of products and services, which seamlessly integrate to provide a cohesive and immersive user experience. This approach not only enhances customer satisfaction and loyalty but also reinforces Apple's reputation as a leader in innovation and design.

Leveraging Emotional Appeal:

In addition to functional benefits, differentiation can also be achieved through emotional appeal, tapping into consumers' aspirations, values, and lifestyle choices. By aligning with the emotional needs and desires of target audiences, brands can forge deeper connections and foster stronger brand loyalty.

Conclusion:

Differentiation is a cornerstone of successful positioning strategies, enabling companies to carve out a distinct identity and competitive advantage in the marketplace. By highlighting unique features, benefits, or attributes that resonate with target customers, businesses can position themselves as leaders in their respective industries and drive sustained growth and profitability.

Chapter 3
Guerrilla Marketing Tactics

Ambush Marketing

Ambush marketing is a strategic tactic used by companies to capitalize on major events or promotions without being an official sponsor. By cleverly associating themselves with popular events or brands, businesses can generate buzz, increase brand visibility, and gain a competitive advantage over their rivals.

Exploiting Regulatory Loopholes:

Ambush marketing often involves exploiting regulatory loopholes to skirt restrictions on official sponsorship rights. This can include tactics such as clever wordplay, guerrilla advertising, or ambush stunts that create the impression of sponsorship without actually violating any laws or regulations.

Example Case Study: Adidas at the 2020 Tokyo Olympics

The 2020 Tokyo Olympics presented a significant opportunity for Adidas, one of the world's leading sports brands, to showcase its products and solidify its position in the global athletic market. With a diverse range of athletes representing various countries and sports, Adidas aimed to leverage this platform to enhance brand visibility, engage with consumers, and drive sales.

Challenges Faced:

Delayed Olympics: The postponement of the 2020 Olympics due to the COVID-19 pandemic posed challenges in terms of marketing strategies and product launches.

Competitive Landscape: Adidas faced fierce competition from other sportswear giants like Nike and Under Armour, requiring innovative strategies to stand out.

Changing Consumer Preferences: Shifts in consumer preferences towards sustainable and ethically produced products necessitated a re-evaluation of Adidas' approach.

Strategies Implemented:

Digital Engagement:

Adidas focused on digital platforms to connect with consumers unable to attend the Olympics in person due to pandemic-related restrictions. This included interactive social media campaigns, virtual events, and live streaming of athlete performances.

Athlete Partnerships:

Collaborating with top athletes competing in the Olympics helped Adidas garner attention and credibility. Endorsements from athletes such as Simone Biles and Naomi Osaka highlighted the brand's commitment to excellence.

Sustainability Initiatives:

Adidas emphasized its sustainability efforts by launching eco-friendly products and promoting responsible manufacturing practices. This resonated with environmentally conscious consumers and enhanced the brand's reputation.

Innovative Product Releases:

Leveraging the Olympic stage, Adidas unveiled innovative products tailored to the needs of athletes. This included advanced sportswear technologies designed to enhance performance and comfort.

Results and Impact:

Increased Brand Awareness:

Adidas' strategic marketing initiatives during the Tokyo Olympics resulted in heightened brand visibility and recognition globally.

Sales Growth:

Despite the challenges posed by the pandemic, Adidas experienced a surge in sales attributed to its Olympic-themed product releases and effective marketing campaigns.

Positive Consumer Perception:

The emphasis on sustainability and athlete partnerships contributed to a positive perception of Adidas among consumers, enhancing brand loyalty and trust.

Competitive Edge:

By differentiating itself through digital engagement, sustainability initiatives, and athlete partnerships, Adidas strengthened its position in the competitive sportswear market.

Conclusion:

The 2020 Tokyo Olympics served as a platform for Adidas to demonstrate its commitment to innovation, sustainability, and athlete empowerment. Through strategic marketing efforts and product launches, Adidas successfully capitalized on the global event to reinforce its brand identity and drive business growth. As the sporting landscape continues to evolve, Adidas remains poised to adapt and thrive in an ever-changing market.

Conclusion:

Ambush marketing is a powerful guerrilla marketing tactic that enables companies to make a splash without the hefty price tag associated with official sponsorship rights. By capitalizing on major events or promotions through creative and unconventional means, businesses can level the playing field and compete effectively against larger, more established rivals.

Chapter 4

Defensive Marketing Strategies

Brand Protection

Brand protection is a critical aspect of defensive marketing strategies, aimed at safeguarding a company's reputation, assets, and market share from competitive threats and external risks. By proactively addressing vulnerabilities and mitigating potential risks, businesses can maintain consumer trust and loyalty while minimizing the impact of adverse events.

Monitoring and Enforcement:

Effective brand protection involves continuous monitoring of market dynamics, competitor actions, and online channels to identify potential threats or infringements. This proactive approach allows companies to detect unauthorized use of their intellectual property, trademarks, or brand assets and take swift action to enforce their rights through legal means or other remedial measures.

Example Case Study: McDonald's and the McLibel Case

McDonald's, a global fast-food giant, faced a significant brand protection challenge in the infamous "McLibel" case. The company found itself embroiled in a high-profile legal battle with activists who accused McDonald's of various unethical practices, including environmental damage, exploitation of workers, and promoting unhealthy food.

Despite the negative publicity and extensive media coverage surrounding the case, McDonald's took a defensive stance to protect its brand reputation and credibility. The company launched a comprehensive public relations campaign to rebut the allegations and reassure customers of its commitment to social responsibility and sustainability.

Building Brand Resilience:

In addition to reactive measures, brand protection also involves proactive strategies aimed at building resilience and strengthening brand equity. This includes investing in brand building initiatives, cultivating positive relationships with stakeholders, and fostering a culture of transparency and accountability.

Conclusion:

Brand protection is an integral component of defensive marketing strategies, essential for safeguarding a company's most valuable asset – its brand reputation. By implementing proactive monitoring and enforcement measures, businesses can mitigate risks, maintain consumer trust, and preserve their competitive advantage in the marketplace.

Chapter 5
Flanking Marketing Strategies

Niche Marketing

Niche marketing is a strategic flanking tactic that involves targeting a specific segment of the market with specialized products or services tailored to meet their unique needs and preferences. By focusing on underserved or overlooked segments, businesses can carve out a competitive niche and establish themselves as leaders in specialized markets.

Identifying Untapped Opportunities:

Niche marketing begins with identifying untapped opportunities within specific market segments where there is limited competition or unmet demand. This requires careful market research and analysis to understand the distinct needs, preferences, and pain points of target customers within the niche.

Example Case Study: Dollar Shave Club

Dollar Shave Club disrupted the traditional razor market with its niche marketing approach, targeting men who were frustrated with the high cost of branded razors and the inconvenience of purchasing them from traditional retailers. By offering affordable subscription-based razor delivery services directly to consumers, Dollar Shave Club tapped into a lucrative niche market and quickly gained traction with its disruptive business model.

Tailoring Products and Messaging:

Successful niche marketing relies on tailoring products, services, and messaging to resonate with the specific needs and preferences of target customers within the niche. This may involve product customization, personalized marketing communications, and niche-focused branding strategies to differentiate offerings and appeal to niche audiences.

Example Case Study: Etsy

Etsy, an online marketplace for handmade and vintage goods, exemplifies the power of niche marketing. By catering to artisans, crafters, and vintage collectors, Etsy has carved out a niche market for unique, handmade products that appeal to a distinct segment of consumers. The platform provides sellers with a specialized marketplace to showcase their products and connect with buyers who value authenticity and craftsmanship. Through its focus on niche markets, Etsy has cultivated a loyal community of buyers and sellers, driving growth and differentiation in the competitive e-commerce landscape.

Establishing Authority and Expertise:

In niche marketing, credibility and expertise are paramount. Businesses must position themselves as authorities within their niche market to build trust and credibility with consumers. This may involve showcasing industry knowledge, providing valuable content or resources, and actively engaging with the niche community through social media, forums, or events. By establishing themselves as trusted experts, companies can enhance their brand reputation and attract loyal customers within the niche market.

Conclusion:

Niche marketing offers businesses a strategic opportunity to differentiate themselves and gain a competitive advantage in specialized market segments. By identifying and serving niche markets with tailored products and messaging, companies can establish strong brand loyalty, drive customer engagement, and achieve sustainable growth in the long term.

Chapter 6
Pre-emptive Marketing Strategies

Product Innovation

Product innovation is a pre-emptive marketing strategy that involves continuously introducing new or improved products to anticipate and meet changing consumer needs and preferences. By staying ahead of the curve and innovating proactively, businesses can maintain a competitive edge in the marketplace and capture market share before competitors have a chance to respond.

Anticipating Consumer Trends:

Successful product innovation begins with a deep understanding of consumer trends, preferences, and emerging market dynamics. By closely monitoring market trends, conducting consumer research, and leveraging data analytics, businesses can identify opportunities for innovation and develop products that align with evolving consumer demands.

Example Case Study: Tesla

Tesla, the electric vehicle pioneer, exemplifies the power of pre-emptive product innovation in the automotive industry. By recognizing the growing demand for sustainable transportation solutions, Tesla disrupted the traditional automotive market with its innovative electric vehicles. From the groundbreaking Model S to the mass-market Model 3, Tesla continuously pushes the boundaries of innovation, setting new standards for performance, range, and technology in the electric vehicle segment.

Creating Competitive Advantage:

Product innovation is not only about introducing new products but also about enhancing existing offerings to maintain relevance and competitiveness. By investing in research and development, fostering a culture of creativity and experimentation, and collaborating with partners and suppliers, businesses can drive continuous innovation and create sustainable competitive advantage in their respective industries.

Embracing Disruption:

In today's fast-paced business environment, pre-emptive marketing strategies often require businesses to embrace disruption and take calculated risks. By challenging conventional wisdom, exploring new technologies, and pushing the boundaries of innovation, companies can position themselves as leaders of change and shape the future of their industries.

Best Case Study: Apple's Pre-emptive Marketing Strategies

Introduction:

Apple Inc., a renowned technology company, is known for its innovative products and pre-emptive marketing strategies that have consistently set it apart in the highly competitive tech industry. This case study examines how Apple utilizes pre-emptive marketing tactics to maintain market leadership and consumer loyalty.

Challenges Faced:

Rapid Technological Advancements: The tech industry is characterized by rapid advancements and fierce competition, requiring companies like Apple to stay ahead of the curve.

Changing Consumer Preferences: Consumer preferences and trends in technology are constantly evolving, necessitating proactive marketing approaches to meet evolving demands.

Competitive Landscape: Apple faces competition from numerous tech giants, including Samsung, Google, and Huawei, necessitating strategic differentiation to maintain market dominance.

Strategies Implemented:

Product Innovation and Secrecy: Apple invests heavily in research and development to innovate new products that anticipate and exceed consumer expectations. The company maintains a veil of secrecy around its upcoming releases, creating anticipation and excitement among consumers.

Brand Image and Ecosystem: Apple cultivates a strong brand image synonymous with quality, reliability, and innovation. Through its ecosystem of products and services, including iPhones, MacBooks, and Apple Watch, the company creates a seamless user experience, fostering brand loyalty and repeat purchases.

Strategic Partnerships and Alliances: Apple strategically partners with other companies, such as Nike for the Apple Watch Nike edition and Disney for Apple TV+, to leverage each other's strengths and reach new audiences.

Targeted Marketing Campaigns: Apple employs targeted marketing campaigns that resonate with specific consumer segments, emphasizing product features, design, and user experience.

Early Adoption of Emerging Technologies: Apple is quick to adopt emerging technologies such as augmented reality (AR), artificial intelligence (AI), and 5G connectivity, positioning itself as an industry leader and catering to future consumer needs.

Results and Impact:

Market Leadership: Apple's pre-emptive marketing strategies have enabled the company to maintain its position as a market leader in the tech industry, consistently outperforming competitors in terms of revenue and market share.

Consumer Loyalty: By consistently delivering innovative products and services that exceed consumer expectations, Apple has fostered a loyal customer base that eagerly anticipates and purchases its offerings.

Revenue Growth: Apple's proactive approach to marketing and product development has resulted in sustained revenue growth, with each new product release generating significant sales and revenue.

Brand Perception: Apple's strong brand image and reputation for quality and innovation have solidified its position as a premium tech brand, allowing it to command higher prices and maintain healthy profit margins.

Conclusion:

Apple's pre-emptive marketing strategies, characterized by product innovation, brand cultivation, strategic partnerships, and targeted campaigns, have been instrumental in maintaining its market leadership and consumer loyalty. By staying ahead of industry trends and anticipating consumer needs, Apple continues to set the standard for excellence in the tech industry. As technology continues to evolve, Apple remains well-positioned to adapt and thrive, leveraging its pre-emptive marketing strategies to sustain its competitive advantage.

Conclusion:

Product innovation is a powerful pre-emptive marketing strategy that enables businesses to anticipate and respond to changing consumer needs and market dynamics. By staying ahead of the curve, continuously introducing new products, and embracing disruption, companies can maintain a competitive edge, drive growth, and future-proof their businesses in an ever-evolving marketplace.

Chapter 7
Defensive Marketing Strategies

Competitive Pricing

Competitive pricing is a defensive marketing strategy aimed at maintaining market share and profitability in the face of aggressive competition. By strategically adjusting pricing strategies to match or undercut competitors' prices, businesses can defend their position in the market and retain price-sensitive customers.

Pricing Intelligence:

Effective competitive pricing begins with thorough analysis of competitors' pricing strategies and market dynamics. By monitoring competitors' prices, promotional offers, and discount strategies, businesses can gain valuable insights into pricing trends and competitive positioning. This intelligence enables companies to make informed pricing decisions and respond quickly to changes in the market landscape.

Example Case Study: Walmart vs. Target

The rivalry between retail giants Walmart and Target exemplifies the importance of competitive pricing in defensive marketing strategies. Both companies employ aggressive pricing tactics to attract customers and gain market share in the highly competitive retail industry. Walmart, known for its "Everyday Low Prices" strategy, focuses on offering the lowest prices on a wide range of products to appeal to budget-conscious shoppers. In response, Target adopts a more selective pricing approach, emphasizing quality and value while offering competitive prices on targeted product categories.

Value-Based Pricing:

While competitive pricing involves matching or undercutting competitors' prices, it's essential for businesses to also consider the value proposition they offer to customers. Value-based pricing takes into account the perceived value of products or services to customers and sets prices accordingly. By highlighting unique features, benefits, or quality attributes, companies can justify premium pricing and differentiate themselves from competitors.

Price-Matching Policies:

To effectively execute competitive pricing strategies, businesses may implement price-matching policies to reassure customers of their commitment to offering the best prices. Price-matching policies allow customers to compare prices and receive refunds or discounts if they find a lower price for the same product elsewhere. This not only helps businesses retain customers but also fosters trust and loyalty by demonstrating transparency and fairness in pricing.

Example (Assumed) Case Study: Defensive Marketing Strategies in the Retail Industry

Introduction:

In the highly competitive landscape of the retail industry, companies often find themselves engaged in aggressive marketing tactics to gain market share and customer loyalty. However, defensive marketing strategies are equally crucial to protect existing market share and mitigate potential threats from competitors. In this case study, we will explore how a leading retail chain implemented defensive marketing strategies to safeguard its position in the market.

Company Background:

Our subject company, let's call it "PeakMart," is a prominent retail chain operating across multiple regions. With a diverse range of products and a strong brand presence, PeakMart has established itself as a preferred shopping destination for millions of customers.

Challenge:

Despite its market leadership, PeakMart faced increasing competition from both traditional brick-and-mortar retailers and e-commerce giants. The emergence of online shopping trends and the expansion of rival retail chains posed a significant threat to PeakMart's market share and profitability. To maintain its competitive edge, PeakMart needed to devise and implement effective defensive marketing strategies.

Defensive Marketing Strategies Implemented:

Customer Loyalty Programs:

PeakMart revamped its loyalty program to enhance customer retention. By offering exclusive discounts, personalized offers, and rewards for frequent purchases, PeakMart incentivized customers to stay loyal to the brand. This not only encouraged repeat business but also deterred customers from switching to competitors.

Price Matching Guarantee:

To combat the pricing strategies of competitors, PeakMart introduced a price matching guarantee. If customers found identical products at lower prices in competitor stores, PeakMart would match the price, ensuring customers received the best value for their purchases. This strategy not only retained price-sensitive customers but also prevented them from exploring alternative shopping options.

Focus on Product Quality and Variety:

Recognizing that product quality plays a pivotal role in customer satisfaction, PeakMart invested in sourcing high-quality products and expanding its product range. By offering a diverse selection of premium-quality merchandise, PeakMart differentiated itself from competitors and attracted discerning customers who valued product excellence.

Localized Marketing Campaigns:

PeakMart implemented localized marketing campaigns to strengthen its connection with regional communities. By tailoring advertisements, promotions, and events to cater to the preferences and cultural nuances of specific geographic areas, PeakMart fostered a sense of belonging among local customers, thereby reinforcing customer loyalty and brand affinity.

Enhanced Customer Service:

PeakMart prioritized customer service excellence as a cornerstone of its defensive marketing strategy. By training staff to deliver personalized assistance, expedite problem resolution, and create memorable shopping experiences, PeakMart ensured that customers received unparalleled service at every touchpoint. This commitment to exceptional customer service not only retained existing customers but also attracted new ones through positive word-of-mouth recommendations.

Results:

Through the implementation of these defensive marketing strategies, PeakMart successfully safeguarded its market share and fortified its competitive position in the retail industry. Customer retention rates increased, and customer satisfaction levels improved significantly. Furthermore, PeakMart experienced sustained revenue growth despite the intensifying competition, underscoring the effectiveness of its defensive marketing initiatives.

This case study demonstrates the importance of defensive marketing strategies in protecting market share and sustaining competitiveness in the retail industry. By prioritizing customer loyalty, product quality, localized engagement, and superior customer service, PeakMart effectively defended its position against competitive threats and continued to thrive in the dynamic retail landscape. As the retail industry evolves, companies must remain vigilant and proactive in implementing defensive marketing strategies to mitigate risks and capitalize on growth opportunities.

Conclusion:

Competitive pricing is a vital component of defensive marketing strategies, enabling businesses to withstand competitive pressures and maintain their market position. By leveraging pricing intelligence, adopting value-based pricing strategies, and implementing price-matching policies, companies can defend against competitors' pricing tactics and retain customer loyalty in the highly competitive marketplace.

Chapter 8
Growth Hacking Strategies

Viral Marketing

Viral marketing is a growth hacking strategy that relies on creating compelling, shareable content that spreads rapidly through word-of-mouth, social media, and online channels. By harnessing the power of social networks and user-generated content, businesses can achieve exponential growth and reach new audiences with minimal investment.

Creating Shareable Content:

The key to successful viral marketing lies in creating content that resonates with target audiences and compels them to share it with their networks. This can include entertaining videos, informative infographics, interactive quizzes, or engaging social media campaigns that evoke emotions and spark conversation. By tapping into trending topics, cultural references, or viral memes, businesses can increase the likelihood of their content going viral and reaching a wider audience.

Example Case Study: Airbnb

Airbnb's "Live There" campaign is a prime example of successful viral marketing in action. The campaign featured a series of short films showcasing local experiences and encouraging travellers to "live like a local" by staying in Airbnb accommodations. The compelling storytelling and authentic portrayal of travel experiences resonated with audiences worldwide, leading to widespread sharing and engagement on social media. As a result, Airbnb saw a significant increase in brand awareness, user engagement, and bookings, driving growth and market expansion.

Leveraging Influencer Partnerships:

In addition to creating shareable content, businesses can leverage influencer partnerships to amplify their viral marketing efforts. Collaborating with influencers who have a large and engaged following allows brands to tap into existing communities and leverage their influence to spread brand messages organically. By selecting influencers whose values align with their brand and target audience, businesses can enhance credibility, reach new audiences, and drive engagement with their viral campaigns.

Measuring and Optimizing Performance:

To maximize the effectiveness of viral marketing campaigns, businesses must continuously monitor and optimize performance metrics to ensure maximum reach and engagement. This includes tracking key performance indicators such as reach, engagement, shares, and conversions, and leveraging analytics tools to identify opportunities for improvement. By iterating on successful tactics and refining strategies based on data-driven insights, businesses can enhance the effectiveness of their viral marketing efforts and drive sustained growth over time.

Case Study: Growth Hacking Strategies in E-Commerce

Introduction:

In the fast-paced world of e-commerce, companies are constantly seeking innovative and cost-effective ways to accelerate their growth. This case study examines how a burgeoning e-commerce startup, "FashionFrenzy," employed growth hacking strategies to rapidly expand its customer base, increase revenue, and establish itself as a prominent player in the fashion industry.

Company Background:

FashionFrenzy is an online fashion retailer specializing in trendy apparel, accessories, and footwear. Launched just two years ago, FashionFrenzy quickly gained traction among fashion enthusiasts with its unique product offerings, competitive pricing, and seamless shopping experience.

Challenge:

Despite initial success, FashionFrenzy faced stiff competition from established e-commerce giants and struggled to gain significant market share. With limited resources for traditional marketing campaigns, FashionFrenzy needed to adopt unconventional growth hacking strategies to drive exponential growth and outpace competitors.

Growth Hacking Strategies Implemented:

1. Referral Program with Incentives:

FashionFrenzy implemented a referral program that rewarded existing customers for referring friends and family. By offering incentives such as discounts, store credits, or free shipping for both the referrer and the referee, FashionFrenzy incentivized word-of-mouth marketing and exponentially expanded its customer base.

2. Viral Content Marketing:

Leveraging the power of social media, FashionFrenzy created compelling and shareable content that resonated with its target audience. From engaging fashion tutorials and styling tips to user-generated content contests, FashionFrenzy encouraged customers to interact with the brand and share content virally, thereby increasing brand visibility and attracting new customers organically.

3. Flash Sales and Limited-Time Offers:

FashionFrenzy leveraged the scarcity principle by regularly hosting flash sales and limited-time offers on select products. By creating a sense of urgency and exclusivity, FashionFrenzy drove impulse purchases and stimulated demand, resulting in rapid sales growth and heightened customer engagement.

4. Data-Driven Optimization:

FashionFrenzy employed data analytics tools to gain valuable insights into customer behaviour, preferences, and purchasing patterns. By analysing data related to website traffic, conversion rates, and customer demographics, FashionFrenzy identified opportunities for optimization and tailored its marketing strategies to maximize effectiveness and ROI.

5. Partnerships and Collaborations:

To expand its reach and tap into new customer segments, FashionFrenzy forged strategic partnerships and collaborations with influencers, bloggers, and complementary brands. By co-hosting events, sponsoring collaborations, and cross-promoting products, FashionFrenzy extended its brand visibility and leveraged the audiences of its partners to drive traffic and sales.

Results:

Through the implementation of these growth hacking strategies, FashionFrenzy achieved remarkable success and experienced exponential growth in a short period. Customer acquisition rates surged, revenue skyrocketed, and FashionFrenzy emerged as a formidable competitor in the e-commerce fashion landscape. The innovative and agile approach to growth hacking enabled FashionFrenzy to outmanoeuvre competitors and establish a loyal customer base while optimizing marketing spend and resources.

Conclusion:

This case study underscores the transformative impact of growth hacking strategies in driving rapid expansion and market penetration in the e-commerce sector.

Viral marketing offers businesses a powerful growth hacking strategy for achieving rapid, exponential growth and reaching new audiences with minimal investment. By creating shareable content, leveraging influencer partnerships, and measuring performance metrics, businesses can amplify their brand reach, drive engagement, and fuel growth in the digital age.

Chapter 9
Repositioning Strategies

Brand Revitalization

Brand revitalization is a repositioning strategy aimed at breathing new life into a stagnant or declining brand by revitalizing its image, offerings, and market perception. By identifying areas of weakness or outdatedness and implementing strategic changes, businesses can reinvigorate their brand and regain relevance in the marketplace.

Assessing Brand Perception:

The first step in brand revitalization is to assess the current perception of the brand among consumers, stakeholders, and the market at large. This involves conducting comprehensive brand audits, market research, and consumer surveys to identify areas where the brand may be falling short or losing relevance. By gaining insights into consumer perceptions, preferences, and competitive positioning, businesses can pinpoint opportunities for improvement and develop a strategic roadmap for revitalization.

Example Case Study: McDonald's "I'm Lovin' It" Campaign

McDonald's successful brand revitalization campaign, "I'm Lovin' It," exemplifies the power of strategic repositioning in revitalizing a brand's image and reconnecting with consumers. In response to shifting consumer preferences and increased competition in the fast-food industry, McDonald's launched the iconic "I'm Lovin' It" campaign, emphasizing positivity, fun, and enjoyment in its brand messaging. The campaign resonated with consumers worldwide, revitalizing the brand's image and driving increased sales and customer loyalty.

Innovating Product Offerings:

Brand revitalization often involves updating or innovating product offerings to better align with changing consumer preferences and market trends. This may include introducing new products or menu items, reformulating existing offerings, or enhancing product features and quality to meet evolving consumer demands. By staying ahead of the curve and continuously innovating, businesses can differentiate their brand and attract new customers while re-engaging existing ones.

Rebranding and Visual Identity:

Rebranding is another common strategy used in brand revitalization efforts, involving the redesign of logos, packaging, marketing materials, and brand messaging to create a fresh and contemporary look and feel. A well-executed rebranding initiative can breathe new life into a brand, signalling to consumers that the brand is evolving and staying relevant in a changing marketplace.

Conclusion:

Brand revitalization is a strategic imperative for businesses looking to stay competitive and relevant in today's dynamic marketplace. By assessing brand perception, innovating product offerings, and rebranding as needed, businesses can revitalize their brand and reignite consumer interest, driving growth and success in the long term.

Chapter 10: Defensive Marketing Strategies

Customer Retention

Customer retention is a defensive marketing strategy focused on nurturing and maintaining relationships with existing customers to ensure long-term loyalty and repeat business. By implementing effective retention tactics, businesses can minimize customer churn, maximize lifetime value, and safeguard against competitive threats.

Building Strong Relationships:

Central to customer retention is building strong, meaningful relationships with customers based on trust, satisfaction, and mutual value. This involves delivering exceptional customer experiences at every touchpoint, from initial purchase to post-sale support. By exceeding customer expectations and demonstrating a commitment to their success and satisfaction, businesses can foster loyalty and advocacy among their customer base.

Example Case Study: Amazon Prime

Amazon Prime's membership program is a prime example of effective customer retention strategy in action. By offering a range of benefits, including free shipping, exclusive deals, and access to streaming content, Amazon incentivizes customers to become Prime members and enjoy ongoing value and convenience. The program not only encourages repeat purchases but also fosters long-term loyalty and engagement, driving sustained revenue growth for Amazon.

Personalization and Customization:

Personalization plays a crucial role in customer retention, allowing businesses to tailor products, services, and communications to individual customer preferences and needs. By leveraging data analytics and customer insights, businesses can deliver personalized recommendations, offers, and experiences that resonate with each customer on a personal level, enhancing satisfaction and loyalty.

Loyalty Programs and Incentives:

Loyalty programs are effective tools for incentivizing repeat business and rewarding loyal customers for their ongoing patronage. By offering rewards, discounts, and exclusive perks to repeat customers, businesses can reinforce loyalty and encourage continued engagement. Well-designed loyalty programs not only increase customer retention but also drive incremental sales and revenue growth over time.

Example Case Study: Defensive Marketing Strategies in the Telecom Industry

Introduction: In the fiercely competitive telecom industry, companies often find themselves engaged in aggressive marketing tactics to gain market share and attract new customers. However, defensive marketing strategies play a crucial role in protecting existing market share and mitigating potential threats from competitors. This case study examines how a leading telecom company,

"TeleConnect," successfully implemented defensive marketing strategies to safeguard its position in the market.

Company Background:

TeleConnect is a major player in the telecom industry, providing a wide range of services including mobile, internet, and landline connections. With a large customer base and a strong brand reputation, TeleConnect has established itself as a trusted provider in the market.

Challenge:

Despite its market leadership, TeleConnect faced increasing competition from both traditional telecom providers and emerging digital disruptors. The introduction of new technologies and the proliferation of alternative communication platforms posed a significant threat to TeleConnect's market share and profitability. To maintain its competitive edge, TeleConnect needed to devise and implement effective defensive marketing strategies.

Defensive Marketing Strategies Implemented:

Customer Retention Programs: TeleConnect revamped its customer retention programs to enhance loyalty among existing customers. By offering exclusive rewards, discounts on service upgrades, and personalized offers tailored to individual usage patterns, TeleConnect incentivized customers to stay with the brand, reducing the likelihood of churn to competitors.

Service Quality Improvements:

Recognizing the importance of service quality in customer satisfaction, TeleConnect invested in infrastructure upgrades and network enhancements to deliver superior performance and reliability. By minimizing service disruptions, improving call quality, and optimizing internet speeds, TeleConnect ensured that customers received a seamless and uninterrupted experience, thereby reducing the temptation to switch to competitors.

Competitive Pricing Strategies:

TeleConnect implemented competitive pricing strategies to retain price-sensitive customers and deter them from switching to lower-cost alternatives. By offering bundled service packages, seasonal promotions, and price match guarantees, TeleConnect provided value for money while maintaining its revenue streams and profitability.

Proactive Customer Service:

TeleConnect prioritized proactive customer service as a key defensive marketing strategy. By establishing dedicated customer support channels, implementing proactive outreach programs, and swiftly addressing customer complaints and inquiries, TeleConnect demonstrated its commitment to customer satisfaction and loyalty, fostering a positive brand reputation in the process.

Strategic Partnerships and Alliances:

To reinforce its market position and expand its service offerings, TeleConnect forged strategic partnerships and alliances with complementary companies in related industries. By offering bundled services, cross-promotional deals, and joint marketing campaigns, TeleConnect extended its reach and diversified its revenue streams, thereby reducing dependence on any single product or service category.

Results:

Through the implementation of these defensive marketing strategies, TeleConnect successfully protected its market share, minimized customer attrition, and sustained its competitive position in the telecom industry. Customer retention rates improved, service quality perceptions strengthened, and TeleConnect maintained a stable revenue trajectory despite the challenges posed by competitors and market dynamics.

Conclusion:

This case study demonstrates the critical role of defensive marketing strategies in safeguarding market share and ensuring long-term viability in the telecom industry. By prioritizing customer retention, service quality, competitive pricing, proactive customer service, and strategic partnerships, TeleConnect effectively defended its position against competitive threats and remained resilient in a dynamic and evolving market landscape.

Customer retention is essential for businesses seeking to maintain a competitive edge and sustain long-term success in today's crowded marketplace. By prioritizing customer relationships, delivering personalized experiences, and implementing loyalty programs, businesses can nurture loyalty, drive repeat business, and fortify their position against competitive threats.

Chapter 11
Street Marketing Tactics

Street Marketing

Street marketing is a guerrilla marketing tactic that involves unconventional, high-impact promotional activities conducted in public spaces to attract attention and generate buzz. By leveraging creativity, novelty, and surprise, businesses can create memorable experiences that resonate with consumers and drive brand awareness.

Creating Memorable Experiences:

Street marketing campaigns are designed to create memorable experiences that captivate and engage consumers in unexpected ways. This can include interactive installations, pop-up events, or immersive brand activations that surprise and delight passersby. By sparking curiosity and fostering emotional connections, street marketing campaigns leave a lasting impression on consumers and increase brand recall.

Example Case Study: Red Bull Stratos

Red Bull's Stratos project is a standout example of successful street marketing that captured global attention and generated widespread buzz. The project involved Austrian skydiver Felix Baumgartner's record-breaking freefall from the stratosphere, sponsored by Red Bull. The event garnered extensive media coverage and social media buzz, showcasing Red Bull's commitment to pushing the limits of human potential and capturing the imagination of millions worldwide.

Leveraging Local Communities:

Street marketing offers businesses the opportunity to connect with local communities and target audiences on a personal level. By tailoring campaigns to reflect the unique characteristics and culture of each location, businesses can resonate more deeply with consumers and foster a sense of belonging and affinity with the brand. Whether through street art, cultural events, or grassroots activations, businesses can strengthen their ties to local communities and build brand loyalty.

Amplifying Reach Through Social Media:

In today's digital age, street marketing campaigns have the added benefit of amplifying reach and engagement through social media channels. By encouraging consumers to share their experiences on social media platforms, businesses can extend the reach of their campaigns and amplify brand visibility. User-generated content and viral sharing further enhance the impact of street marketing initiatives, driving organic reach and engagement.

Conclusion:

Street marketing is a powerful guerrilla marketing tactic that allows businesses to cut through the clutter and capture consumers' attention in a crowded marketplace. By creating memorable experiences, leveraging local communities, and amplifying reach through social media, businesses can drive brand awareness, foster engagement, and leave a lasting impression on consumers.

Chapter 12
Repositioning Strategies

Brand Extension

Brand extension is a repositioning strategy that involves leveraging the equity and goodwill of an existing brand to introduce new products or enter new markets. By extending the brand into related or complementary categories, businesses can capitalize on their existing brand recognition and customer loyalty to drive growth and expand their market reach.

Leveraging Brand Equity:

Brand extension relies on the strength of the existing brand to create credibility and acceptance for new offerings in the marketplace. By leveraging the positive associations, reputation, and trust built around the core brand, businesses can minimize the risks associated with launching new products or entering unfamiliar markets. This allows them to capitalize on existing customer relationships and drive sales through cross-promotion and upselling.

Example Case Study: Dove's Brand Extension

Dove, known for its range of beauty and personal care products, successfully extended its brand into the skincare category with the launch of Dove Men+Care. Leveraging its reputation for gentle, nourishing formulations, Dove capitalized on the growing demand for men's grooming products and positioned itself as a trusted brand for men's skincare needs. The brand extension not only expanded Dove's product portfolio but also reinforced its commitment to inclusive beauty and self-care across genders.

Expanding Market Reach:

Brand extension enables businesses to enter new markets or target new customer segments by diversifying their product offerings. By identifying synergies between the core brand and adjacent categories, businesses can tap into untapped market opportunities and capture additional market share. This allows them to extend their brand presence and relevance across a broader spectrum of consumer needs and preferences.

Building on Brand Trust:

One of the primary advantages of brand extension is the ability to build on existing brand trust and credibility. Consumers are more likely to try new products or services from a brand they already know and trust. By extending the brand into related or complementary categories, businesses can mitigate the perceived risk associated with trying something new, thereby increasing the likelihood of adoption and acceptance by consumers.

Example Case Study: Apple

Apple is a master of brand extension, continually expanding its product portfolio while maintaining a strong brand identity. From computers to smartphones, tablets, wearables, and services like

Apple Music and Apple TV+, Apple has successfully extended its brand into diverse product categories. Each new offering benefits from the association with Apple's reputation for innovation, design excellence, and user experience, allowing the company to command premium pricing and maintain customer loyalty across its ecosystem of products and services.

Leveraging Economies of Scope:

Brand extension can also offer economic benefits through economies of scope. By leveraging existing resources, capabilities, and distribution channels, businesses can achieve cost efficiencies and economies of scale when introducing new products under an established brand. This can result in lower marketing costs, faster time to market, and increased profitability for brand extensions compared to launching entirely new brands from scratch.

Managing Brand Dilution:

While brand extension offers many advantages, it also carries the risk of brand dilution if not executed carefully. Introducing unrelated or inconsistent products under an established brand can confuse consumers and erode brand equity over time. Therefore, it's crucial for businesses to maintain brand coherence and relevance when extending their brand into new categories, ensuring that the new offerings align with the core values, positioning, and target audience of the original brand.

Managing Brand Consistency:

While brand extension offers opportunities for growth and diversification, it's essential for businesses to maintain consistency and coherence across their brand portfolio. Consistency in brand positioning, messaging, and visual identity ensures that consumers perceive the brand extension as a natural extension of the core brand and reinforces brand equity and recognition. By upholding brand values and standards, businesses can preserve customer trust and loyalty while successfully expanding into new markets.

Conclusion:

Brand extension is a strategic repositioning strategy that allows businesses to leverage the equity of their existing brand to drive growth and expand into new markets. By capitalizing on brand recognition, customer loyalty, and market insights, businesses can introduce new products or enter new categories with confidence, ultimately strengthening their competitive position and fuelling long-term success.

In conclusion, marketing warfare encompasses a range of strategic tactics and manoeuvres aimed at gaining a competitive advantage in the marketplace. From offensive strategies like differentiation and viral marketing to defensive tactics such as competitive pricing and customer retention, businesses have a multitude of tools at their disposal to navigate the competitive landscape and drive growth.

Throughout this book, we've explored various marketing warfare techniques, each with its own set of principles, case studies, and practical applications. Whether seeking to capture market share, defend against rivals, or reposition a brand for success, businesses can draw inspiration from the strategies outlined in these chapters to craft their own battle plans and achieve their objectives.

In today's fast-paced and ever-changing business environment, mastering marketing warfare is essential for staying ahead of the competition and seizing opportunities for growth. By understanding the dynamics of the marketplace, identifying strategic openings, and deploying the right tactics at the right time, businesses can outmanoeuvre rivals, delight customers, and achieve sustainable success in the long run.

As you continue your journey in the world of marketing, remember the lessons learned from this book and apply them thoughtfully and strategically in your own endeavours. With creativity, perseverance, and a willingness to adapt, you can conquer challenges, capitalize on opportunities, and emerge victorious in the ongoing battle for market supremacy.

Thank you for joining us on this exploration of marketing warfare techniques. May the insights gained here serve as valuable weapons in your arsenal as you navigate the competitive landscape and strive for success in your business endeavours.

PART- TWO

Marketing Warfare in Digital Era

Marketing Warfare in Digital Era

Introduction

In today's digital age, the battleground for market dominance has shifted to the online realm, where businesses must adapt their strategies to thrive in a landscape defined by rapid technological advancements, evolving consumer behaviours, and fierce competition. Marketing warfare tactics, originally coined by Al Ries and Jack Trout in the 1980s, remain relevant but have undergone significant transformation in response to the digital revolution.

This Part of the book, "Marketing Warfare in Digital Era," delves into the intricacies of modern marketing warfare strategies tailored for the digital landscape. From offensive manoeuvres to defensive tactics, each chapter explores a different aspect of digital marketing warfare, providing insights, case studies, and practical guidance for navigating the complexities of the digital battlefield.

Throughout these pages, readers will discover how to leverage the power of digital technologies, data analytics, and online platforms to outmanoeuvre competitors, capture market share, and achieve sustainable growth in the digital era. Whether you're a seasoned marketing professional or a business owner looking to sharpen your competitive edge, this book offers invaluable insights and strategies for success in today's digital marketplace.

Now, let's embark on a journey through the realms of digital marketing warfare, where innovation, agility, and strategic thinking reign supreme.

Chapter 1

Understanding the Digital Battlefield

In the digital era, the battlefield for market dominance is no longer confined to traditional channels but extends across the vast expanse of the internet. In this chapter, we explore the nuances of the digital battlefield, including key players, emerging trends, and strategic considerations for success.

The Rise of Digital Platforms:

Digital platforms have emerged as the new battlegrounds where businesses compete for consumer attention, engagement, and loyalty. From social media networks like Facebook, Instagram, and Twitter to e-commerce platforms such as Amazon and Alibaba, digital platforms offer unparalleled opportunities for brands to connect with audiences and drive business outcomes.

The Power of Data and Analytics:

In the digital era, data is king, providing businesses with unprecedented insights into consumer behaviours, preferences, and trends. By harnessing the power of data analytics, businesses can gain a deeper understanding of their target audience, optimize marketing strategies, and measure the effectiveness of their campaigns with precision.

The Evolution of Consumer Behaviour:

The digital revolution has transformed consumer behaviour, giving rise to new patterns of interaction, decision-making, and purchasing habits. From the proliferation of mobile devices to the rise of e-commerce and the sharing economy, consumers are more empowered, informed, and demanding than ever before, presenting both challenges and opportunities for businesses.

Strategic Considerations for the Digital Battlefield:

Navigating the digital battlefield requires a strategic approach that takes into account the unique dynamics of the online landscape. From developing a robust digital marketing strategy to mastering the art of content creation, community engagement, and influencer marketing, businesses must adapt their tactics to stay ahead of the competition and win the hearts and minds of digital consumers.

Conclusion:

As businesses continue to navigate the complexities of the digital landscape, understanding the dynamics of the digital battlefield is essential for success. By embracing digital platforms, harnessing the power of data and analytics, and adapting to evolving consumer behaviours, businesses can position themselves for success in the digital era.

Chapter 2

Offensive Strategies in the Digital Arena

In the digital arena, offensive strategies are essential for businesses aiming to gain a competitive edge and seize opportunities for growth. In this chapter, we explore various offensive strategies tailored for the digital landscape, including differentiation, content marketing, and search engine optimization (SEO).

Differentiation in the Digital Age:

In a crowded digital marketplace, differentiation is key to standing out from the competition and capturing the attention of consumers. By identifying unique selling points, communicating value propositions effectively, and creating memorable brand experiences, businesses can differentiate themselves from competitors and establish a distinct identity in the minds of consumers.

Content Marketing as a Weapon:

Content marketing has emerged as a powerful offensive strategy for businesses looking to attract, engage, and convert audiences in the digital age. By creating valuable, relevant, and shareable content across various digital channels, businesses can position themselves as thought leaders, build brand credibility, and drive customer engagement and loyalty over time.

Mastering Search Engine Optimization (SEO):

In the digital era, visibility on search engines is crucial for driving organic traffic and capturing the attention of potential customers. Search engine optimization (SEO) involves optimizing website content, structure, and performance to improve search engine rankings and increase visibility in search results. By mastering the art of SEO, businesses can enhance their online presence, attract qualified leads, and drive conversions at scale.

Leveraging Digital Advertising:

Digital advertising offers businesses a powerful tool for reaching targeted audiences, driving brand awareness, and generating leads and sales. From pay-per-click (PPC) advertising on search engines to display ads, social media ads, and native advertising, businesses can leverage a variety of digital advertising channels to amplify their reach, target specific demographics, and achieve their marketing objectives with precision.

Conclusion:

In the digital arena, offensive strategies are essential for businesses seeking to gain a competitive advantage and achieve their growth objectives. By embracing differentiation, content marketing, SEO, and digital advertising, businesses can position themselves for success in the digital age and capitalize on the vast opportunities presented by the digital landscape.

Chapter 3
Defensive Tactics for Digital Resilience

In the ever-evolving digital landscape, businesses must employ defensive tactics to protect their market position, safeguard against competitive threats, and maintain resilience in the face of challenges. In this chapter, we explore defensive strategies tailored for the digital era, including brand monitoring, reputation management, and cybersecurity measures.

Brand Monitoring and Reputation Management:

Brand monitoring involves actively tracking mentions, discussions, and sentiments about a brand across digital channels, including social media, review platforms, and news websites. By monitoring brand mentions in real-time, businesses can identify potential issues, respond to customer feedback promptly, and mitigate reputational risks before they escalate.

Reputation management is the proactive management of a brand's image and perception in the digital realm. By cultivating positive relationships with customers, addressing negative feedback transparently, and actively seeking to build trust and credibility, businesses can enhance their reputation and strengthen customer loyalty in the digital age.

Cybersecurity Measures to Protect Digital Assets:

As businesses increasingly rely on digital technologies to operate and conduct business, cybersecurity has become a critical concern. Cybersecurity measures aim to protect digital assets, including websites, databases, and customer information, from cyber threats such as data breaches, malware attacks, and phishing scams. By implementing robust cybersecurity protocols, including encryption, firewalls, and multi-factor authentication, businesses can safeguard their digital assets and maintain the trust of their customers.

Legal and Compliance Strategies:

In the digital age, businesses must also navigate a complex landscape of legal and regulatory requirements, including privacy laws, data protection regulations, and intellectual property rights. By staying informed about relevant laws and regulations, implementing compliance measures, and conducting regular audits, businesses can mitigate legal risks and ensure compliance with applicable laws, safeguarding against potential legal liabilities and reputational damage.

Conclusion:

Defensive tactics are essential for businesses seeking to maintain resilience and protect their interests in the digital era. By implementing brand monitoring, reputation management, cybersecurity measures, and legal and compliance strategies, businesses can defend against threats, mitigate risks, and maintain trust and credibility with their customers and stakeholders in the digital age.

Chapter 4

Targeting and Personalization Strategies

In the digital era, targeting and personalization strategies play a crucial role in engaging audiences, driving conversions, and building long-term customer relationships. In this chapter, we delve into the intricacies of targeting and personalization in the digital landscape, including segmentation, behavioural targeting, and dynamic content customization.

Segmentation for Precision Targeting:

Segmentation involves dividing a target audience into distinct groups based on shared characteristics, preferences, or behaviours. By segmenting audiences effectively, businesses can tailor their marketing messages, offers, and experiences to resonate with specific segments, increasing relevance and engagement. Common segmentation criteria include demographics, psychographics, geographic location, and past purchase behaviour.

Behavioural Targeting for Enhanced Relevance:

Behavioural targeting leverages user data and online behaviours to deliver personalized content and advertising experiences to individual users. By tracking user interactions, browsing history, and online activities, businesses can infer user preferences, interests, and intent, enabling them to deliver targeted messages and offers at the right time and place. Behavioural targeting enhances relevance, improves ad performance, and increases the likelihood of conversion.

Dynamic Content Customization:

Dynamic content customization involves dynamically adapting website content, email campaigns, or digital ads based on user attributes, behaviours, or preferences. By serving personalized content to individual users, businesses can create more engaging and relevant experiences, driving higher levels of interaction and conversion. Dynamic content customization techniques include product recommendations, personalized email subject lines, and tailored website experiences based on user history.

Omnichannel Personalization for Seamless Experiences:

Omnichannel personalization aims to deliver cohesive and consistent experiences across multiple digital touchpoints, including websites, mobile apps, social media platforms, and email. By leveraging data and insights from various channels, businesses can personalize interactions and messaging at each touchpoint, creating seamless and personalized experiences that delight customers and drive loyalty.

These strategies are essential for businesses seeking to engage audiences, drive conversions, and build lasting relationships in the digital age. By leveraging Them, businesses can deliver relevant, personalized experiences that resonate with consumers and drive business outcomes in the competitive digital landscape.

Chapter 5
Content Marketing Mastery

Content marketing has emerged as a cornerstone of digital marketing strategies, allowing businesses to attract, engage, and convert audiences through valuable and relevant content. In this chapter, we delve into the principles, tactics, and best practices for mastering content marketing in the digital era.

Understanding the Power of Content:

Content serves as the foundation of digital marketing efforts, enabling businesses to educate, entertain, and inspire audiences across various digital channels. Whether through blog posts, videos, infographics, or social media posts, high-quality content helps businesses establish thought leadership, build brand credibility, and foster trust with their target audience.

Developing a Content Strategy:

A successful content marketing strategy begins with a clear understanding of audience needs, preferences, and pain points. Businesses must define their target audience personas, identify relevant topics and themes, and establish key performance indicators (KPIs) to measure success. A well-defined content strategy guides content creation, distribution, and optimization efforts, ensuring alignment with business goals and audience interests.

Creating Compelling Content:

Compelling content is essential for capturing and retaining audience attention in the crowded digital landscape. Businesses must focus on creating content that is informative, entertaining, and actionable, providing value to the audience and addressing their needs and interests. From storytelling to visual storytelling, businesses can leverage various content formats and techniques to engage audiences and drive desired outcomes.

Distributing and Amplifying Content:

Content distribution is key to reaching a wider audience and maximizing the impact of content marketing efforts. Businesses must identify relevant channels and platforms where their target audience congregates, whether it's social media, email newsletters, industry forums, or third-party publications. By amplifying content through strategic distribution tactics, businesses can increase visibility, engagement, and conversions.

Measuring and Optimizing Performance:

Measuring the effectiveness of content marketing efforts is essential for optimizing performance and driving continuous improvement. Businesses should track key metrics such as website traffic, engagement metrics, lead generation, and conversion rates to gauge the impact of their content and identify areas for optimization. By analysing data and insights, businesses can refine their content strategy

Chapter 6

Harnessing the Power of Social Media Marketing

Social media has revolutionized the way businesses connect with consumers, enabling them to engage in real-time conversations, build communities, and drive brand awareness and loyalty. In this chapter, we explore the strategies, tactics, and best practices for harnessing the power of social media marketing in the digital era.

Understanding Social Media Platforms:

Social media platforms offer diverse opportunities for businesses to connect with their target audience, including Facebook, Instagram, Twitter, LinkedIn, Pinterest, TikTok, and more. Each platform has its own unique characteristics, demographics, and user behaviours, requiring businesses to tailor their strategies and content to fit the platform and audience.

Crafting a Social Media Strategy:

A successful social media strategy begins with clear objectives, target audience identification, and platform selection. Businesses must define their goals, whether it's brand awareness, lead generation, customer engagement, or sales, and develop content and tactics to achieve those goals effectively. A well-defined social media strategy guides content creation, posting frequency, engagement tactics, and performance measurement.

Content Creation and Curation:

Compelling content is essential for capturing audience attention and driving engagement on social media. Businesses should focus on creating a mix of content types, including images, videos, infographics, blog posts, user-generated content, and interactive content, to keep their audience engaged and entertained. Content should be relevant, informative, entertaining, and aligned with the brand's tone and personality.

Engaging with the Audience:

Social media is inherently social, requiring businesses to actively engage with their audience through likes, comments, shares, and direct messages. By responding promptly to inquiries, addressing customer feedback, and participating in relevant conversations, businesses can build trust, foster relationships, and strengthen brand loyalty on social media.

Leveraging Social Advertising:

Social media advertising offers businesses a powerful tool for reaching targeted audiences, driving conversions, and achieving marketing objectives. From sponsored posts and ads to carousel ads, video ads, and influencer partnerships, businesses can leverage a variety of ad formats and targeting options to reach their ideal customers and maximize their return on investment.

Analysing and Optimizing Performance:

Measuring the effectiveness of social media marketing efforts is essential for optimizing performance and driving continuous improvement. Businesses should track key metrics such as reach, engagement, click-through rates, conversion rates, and return on ad spend (ROAS) to gauge the impact of their social media activities and identify areas for optimization. By analysing data and insights, businesses can refine their social media strategy, improve content quality, and enhance overall performance.

Conclusion:

Social media marketing presents immense opportunities for businesses to connect with consumers, build brand awareness, and drive business results in the digital age. By understanding the unique dynamics of each social media platform, crafting a tailored strategy, creating compelling content, engaging with the audience, leveraging social advertising, and analysing performance, businesses can harness the power of social media to achieve their marketing objectives and thrive in the competitive digital landscape.

Chapter 7

Email Marketing Excellence

Email marketing remains one of the most effective and reliable digital marketing channels for businesses to engage with their audience, nurture leads, and drive conversions. In this chapter, we delve into the strategies, tactics, and best practices for achieving email marketing excellence in the digital era.

Building an Engaged Subscriber List:

The foundation of successful email marketing lies in building a high-quality subscriber list of engaged and interested recipients. Businesses should employ strategies such as offering valuable incentives, creating compelling opt-in forms, and segmenting subscribers based on their interests and behaviours to attract and retain subscribers who are genuinely interested in their content and offerings.

Crafting Compelling Email Content:

Compelling email content is essential for capturing the attention of subscribers and driving desired actions. Businesses should focus on creating personalized, relevant, and valuable content that resonates with their audience's interests, pain points, and preferences. Whether it's newsletters, promotional offers, educational content, or event invitations, every email should provide value and compel recipients to take action.

Optimizing Email Design and Layout:

Email design and layout play a crucial role in the success of email marketing campaigns. Businesses should focus on creating visually appealing, mobile-responsive emails that are easy to read and navigate on any device. Attention-grabbing subject lines, clear calls-to-action (CTAs), and concise yet compelling copy are essential elements of effective email design that drive engagement and conversions.

Automating Email Campaigns:

Email automation allows businesses to streamline their email marketing efforts, deliver timely and relevant messages, and nurture leads through the sales funnel efficiently. Businesses can leverage automation tools to set up drip campaigns, welcome sequences, abandoned cart reminders, and personalized workflows based on subscriber actions and behaviours, increasing engagement and driving conversions.

Measuring and Analysing Email Performance:

Measuring the effectiveness of email marketing campaigns is essential for optimizing performance and driving continuous improvement. Businesses should track key metrics such as open rates, click-through rates, conversion rates, and email deliverability to gauge the impact of their campaigns and identify areas for optimization. By analysing data and insights, businesses can refine their email marketing strategy, improve targeting and segmentation, and enhance overall performance.

Compliance and Best Practices:

In addition to delivering engaging content and driving results, businesses must also adhere to email marketing best practices and legal regulations to maintain trust and credibility with subscribers. This includes obtaining explicit consent from subscribers, providing easy opt-out options, and complying with anti-spam laws such as the CAN-SPAM Act and GDPR (General Data Protection Regulation).

Conclusion:

Email marketing continues to be a powerful tool for businesses to connect with their audience, drive engagement, and achieve their marketing objectives in the digital age. By focusing on building an engaged subscriber list, crafting compelling content, optimizing design and layout, automating campaigns, measuring performance, and adhering to best practices, businesses can achieve email marketing excellence and unlock the full potential of this valuable marketing channel.

Chapter 8

Search Engine Optimization (SEO) Mastery

Search engine optimization (SEO) remains a critical component of digital marketing strategies, enabling businesses to improve their online visibility, drive organic traffic, and enhance their overall digital presence. In this chapter, we explore the strategies, techniques, and best practices for mastering SEO in the digital era.

Understanding the Fundamentals of SEO:

SEO involves optimizing websites and content to rank higher in search engine results pages (SERPs) for relevant keywords and phrases. Businesses must understand the key elements of SEO, including on-page optimization, off-page optimization, technical SEO, and user experience (UX), to improve their search engine rankings and attract more organic traffic.

Keyword Research and Analysis:

Keyword research is the foundation of effective SEO, helping businesses identify the terms and phrases their target audience is searching for online. By conducting thorough keyword research and analysis, businesses can uncover valuable insights into search intent, competition levels, and content opportunities, allowing them to optimize their content strategy and target high-value keywords with the potential for maximum impact.

On-Page Optimization Techniques:

On-page optimization involves optimizing individual web pages to improve their relevance, visibility, and ranking in search engine results. Businesses should focus on optimizing meta tags, headings, content, images, and URLs for target keywords, while also ensuring a seamless user experience and fast page loading times. By implementing on-page optimization techniques, businesses can enhance their website's search engine visibility and attract more organic traffic.

Off-Page SEO Strategies:

Off-page SEO refers to activities conducted outside of the website to improve its search engine rankings and authority. This includes building high-quality backlinks from authoritative websites, earning mentions and citations from reputable sources, and cultivating a strong social media presence. Off-page SEO signals indicate to search engines that a website is credible, trustworthy, and relevant, leading to higher rankings and increased organic traffic.

Technical SEO Best Practices:

Technical SEO focuses on optimizing the technical aspects of a website to improve its crawlability, indexability, and overall performance in search engine rankings. This includes optimizing website structure, navigation, URL structure, and internal linking, as well as addressing issues such as duplicate content, broken links, and page speed. By implementing technical SEO best practices, businesses can ensure that their website is optimized for search engines and provides a positive user experience.

Measuring and Monitoring SEO Performance:

Measuring the effectiveness of SEO efforts is essential for tracking progress, identifying areas for improvement, and maximizing return on investment. Businesses should track key metrics such as organic traffic, keyword rankings, backlink profile, and conversion rates to gauge the impact of their SEO strategies and tactics. By monitoring performance metrics and analysing data insights, businesses can refine their SEO approach, optimize content, and achieve sustainable long-term results.

Conclusion:

Mastering SEO is essential for businesses looking to improve their online visibility, attract more organic traffic, and achieve their marketing objectives in the digital age. By understanding the fundamentals of SEO, conducting comprehensive keyword research, implementing on-page and off-page optimization techniques, optimizing technical aspects, and measuring performance, businesses can achieve SEO mastery and position themselves for success in the competitive digital landscape.

Chapter 9

Pay-Per-Click (PPC) Advertising Strategies

Pay-per-click (PPC) advertising is a powerful digital marketing channel that allows businesses to reach their target audience with precision, drive traffic to their websites, and achieve their marketing objectives through paid ads. In this chapter, we explore the strategies, tactics, and best practices for leveraging PPC advertising effectively in the digital era.

Understanding PPC Advertising:

PPC advertising involves advertisers paying a fee each time their ad is clicked, making it a cost-effective and measurable way to drive targeted traffic to websites. Platforms like Google Ads, Bing Ads, and social media advertising platforms offer robust PPC advertising solutions that allow businesses to reach their audience based on demographics, interests, and search intent.

Setting PPC Campaign Objectives:

Before launching a PPC campaign, businesses must define clear objectives and key performance indicators (KPIs) to measure success. Whether the goal is to increase website traffic, generate leads, drive conversions, or boost brand awareness, aligning PPC campaign objectives with broader marketing goals ensures that resources are invested wisely and campaigns deliver tangible results.

Keyword Research and Selection:

Keyword research is a critical component of PPC advertising, helping businesses identify relevant search terms and phrases that their target audience is using to find products or services. By conducting comprehensive keyword research and selection, businesses can identify high-intent keywords, assess competition levels, and optimize their PPC campaigns for maximum impact and return on investment.

Crafting Compelling Ad Copy:

Compelling ad copy is essential for capturing audience attention, driving clicks, and achieving campaign objectives. Businesses should focus on creating ad copy that is clear, concise, and compelling, highlighting unique selling propositions, benefits, and calls-to-action (CTAs) that resonate with their target audience. A/B testing different ad variations helps identify the most effective messaging and optimize campaign performance over time.

Targeting and Audience Segmentation:

Effective audience targeting and segmentation are key to maximizing the impact of PPC advertising campaigns. Businesses can leverage targeting options such as demographics, interests, geographic location, and device type to reach their ideal audience segments with precision. By segmenting audiences and tailoring ad messaging to specific demographics or user behaviours, businesses can increase relevance and drive higher conversion rates.

Budgeting and Bid Management:

Budgeting and bid management are crucial aspects of PPC advertising, ensuring that businesses allocate resources effectively and optimize campaign performance. Businesses should set realistic budgets based on campaign objectives, monitor spending closely, and adjust bids and targeting parameters to maximize return on investment. Continuous monitoring and optimization help businesses achieve optimal campaign performance and maximize their advertising budget's effectiveness.

Measuring and Analysing PPC Performance:

Measuring the effectiveness of PPC campaigns is essential for evaluating performance, identifying areas for improvement, and optimizing campaign strategies. Businesses should track key performance metrics such as click-through rates (CTR), conversion rates, cost per click (CPC), return on ad spend (ROAS), and quality score to assess campaign performance and make data-driven decisions to optimize future campaigns.

Conclusion:

PPC advertising offers businesses a powerful and scalable way to reach their target audience, drive traffic, and achieve marketing objectives in the digital era. By understanding the fundamentals of

PPC advertising, setting clear campaign objectives, conducting keyword research, crafting compelling ad copy, targeting and segmenting audiences effectively, managing budgets and bids strategically, and measuring performance, businesses can leverage PPC advertising to drive growth and success in the competitive digital landscape.

Chapter 10

Conversion Rate Optimization (CRO) Tactics

Conversion rate optimization (CRO) is a crucial aspect of digital marketing that focuses on maximizing the percentage of website visitors who take desired actions, such as making a purchase, filling out a form, or subscribing to a newsletter. In this chapter, we explore the strategies, tactics, and best practices for optimizing conversion rates and driving business growth in the digital era.

Understanding Conversion Rate Optimization:

Conversion rate optimization (CRO) involves systematically optimizing various elements of a website or landing page to encourage visitors to take specific actions. By analysing user behaviour, conducting A/B tests, and implementing data-driven changes, businesses can improve conversion rates, increase revenue, and maximize the return on investment (ROI) from their digital marketing efforts.

Conducting User Research:

Effective CRO starts with a deep understanding of the target audience's needs, preferences, and behaviours. Businesses should conduct user research through methods such as surveys, interviews, and website analytics to gain insights into user motivations, pain points, and barriers to conversion. Understanding user psychology and decision-making processes enables businesses to design more effective conversion experiences that resonate with their audience.

Optimizing Website Design and User Experience:

Website design and user experience (UX) play a critical role in influencing conversion rates. Businesses should focus on creating intuitive navigation, clear calls-to-action (CTAs), and persuasive landing pages that guide visitors towards desired actions. Mobile optimization is also crucial, as an increasing number of users access websites from smartphones and tablets. By optimizing website design and UX, businesses can reduce friction, improve usability, and increase conversion rates.

Implementing A/B Testing and Experimentation:

A/B testing is a fundamental technique in CRO that involves comparing two or more versions of a webpage or element to determine which performs better in terms of conversion rate. Businesses can test different headlines, CTAs, layouts, and images to identify elements that resonate most with their audience and drive higher conversion rates. Continuous experimentation and optimization help businesses refine their conversion strategies and achieve incremental improvements over time.

Personalizing the User Experience:

Personalization is a powerful strategy for increasing engagement and conversions by delivering tailored experiences to individual users based on their preferences, behaviour, and past interactions. Businesses can leverage data such as browsing history, purchase behaviour, and demographic information to personalize content, product recommendations, and offers. Personalized experiences create a sense of relevance and urgency, driving higher conversion rates and customer satisfaction.

Optimizing Conversion Funnels:

Analysing and optimizing conversion funnels is essential for identifying bottlenecks and optimizing the user journey towards conversion. Businesses should use tools like Google Analytics to track user behaviour at each stage of the funnel, identify drop-off points, and implement improvements to streamline the conversion process. By removing obstacles and friction points, businesses can increase the likelihood of visitors completing desired actions and achieving conversion goals.

Conclusion:

Conversion rate optimization (CRO) is a continuous process of refining and improving the user experience to maximize conversions and drive business growth. By understanding user behaviour, optimizing website design and UX, conducting A/B testing and experimentation, personalizing the user experience, and optimizing conversion funnels, businesses can increase conversion rates, generate more leads, and ultimately achieve their marketing objectives in the competitive digital landscape.

Chapter 11

Reputation Management in the Digital Age

In the digital age, maintaining a positive online reputation is crucial for businesses to build trust, credibility, and goodwill among their target audience. In this chapter, we delve into the strategies, tactics, and best practices for effective reputation management in the digital era.

Understanding Online Reputation Management:

Online reputation management (ORM) involves monitoring, influencing, and managing the perception of a brand or individual across various online channels. It encompasses activities such as monitoring online mentions, responding to customer reviews and feedback, addressing negative publicity, and proactively managing brand image and reputation.

Monitoring Online Mentions and Feedback:

Monitoring online mentions and feedback is the first step in effective reputation management. Businesses should use monitoring tools and social media listening platforms to track brand mentions, customer reviews, and conversations happening across the web. By staying informed about what customers are saying about their brand, businesses can address issues promptly and proactively manage their online reputation.

Responding to Customer Reviews and Feedback:

Customer reviews and feedback can significantly impact a business's reputation and influence purchase decisions. Businesses should actively engage with customers by responding to reviews, both positive and negative, in a timely and professional manner. Acknowledging positive feedback shows appreciation for customer support, while addressing negative feedback demonstrates a commitment to customer satisfaction and willingness to resolve issues.

Addressing Negative Publicity:

Negative publicity or online attacks can tarnish a business's reputation if left unaddressed. Businesses should have a plan in place to address negative publicity promptly and effectively. This may involve issuing public statements, addressing concerns directly with affected parties, and taking appropriate action to rectify any issues. Transparency, honesty, and accountability are key principles in managing negative publicity and preserving brand reputation.

Proactively Managing Brand Image:

Proactively managing brand image involves shaping the narrative surrounding a brand and influencing public perception through strategic communication and branding initiatives. Businesses should focus on building a strong brand identity, communicating core values and messaging consistently across all channels, and showcasing positive aspects of their brand through storytelling and content marketing efforts.

Leveraging Positive Public Relations:

Positive public relations (PR) efforts play a vital role in shaping public perception and enhancing brand reputation. Businesses should actively seek opportunities to generate positive media coverage, participate in industry events and awards, and cultivate relationships with influencers, journalists, and thought leaders in their industry. By positioning themselves as industry leaders and trusted authorities, businesses can enhance their reputation and credibility among their target audience.

Monitoring and Responding to Crisis Situations:

In today's fast-paced digital landscape, crisis situations can arise suddenly and have a significant impact on a business's reputation. Businesses should have a crisis management plan in place, including designated spokespeople, communication protocols, and response strategies. By monitoring online conversations, identifying potential issues early, and responding swiftly and transparently during crises, businesses can mitigate reputational damage and preserve trust and goodwill among stakeholders.

Conclusion:

Effective reputation management is essential for businesses to maintain a positive brand image, build trust with customers, and thrive in the digital age. By actively monitoring online mentions and feedback, responding to customer reviews and feedback, addressing negative publicity, proactively managing brand image, leveraging positive public relations, and preparing for crisis situations, businesses can protect and enhance their reputation and position themselves for long-term success in the competitive digital landscape.

Chapter 12
Influencer Marketing

Influencer marketing is a powerful strategy in the digital age, leveraging the influence of individuals with large and engaged followings to promote products, services, or brands. In this form of marketing, businesses collaborate with influencers—individuals who have established credibility, authority, and a loyal audience within a specific niche or industry—to reach and engage their target audience authentically.

The essence of influencer marketing lies in the trust and authenticity that influencers have built with their followers. Unlike traditional advertising, which often feels impersonal and sales-driven, influencer marketing relies on the genuine connections between influencers and their followers. When an influencer recommends a product or service, their audience is more likely to trust and act upon that recommendation, leading to higher conversion rates and brand engagement.

Influencer marketing can take many forms, including sponsored content, product reviews, brand partnerships, affiliate marketing, and influencer takeovers. The key is to find influencers whose values, interests, and audience align with those of the brand, ensuring that the partnership feels organic and authentic to both the influencer and their followers.

One of the major benefits of influencer marketing is its ability to reach highly targeted audiences. By collaborating with influencers who cater to specific demographics or interests, businesses can ensure that their message resonates with the right audience segments, leading to more meaningful interactions and higher return on investment.

In addition to driving brand awareness and engagement, influencer marketing can also boost credibility and social proof for businesses. When consumers see influencers, they trust endorsing a product or brand, it reinforces their perception of the brand's credibility and quality, leading to increased trust and confidence in their purchasing decisions.

However, like any marketing strategy, influencer marketing requires careful planning, execution, and measurement to be successful. Businesses must identify the right influencers, negotiate terms and agreements, provide clear guidelines and expectations, and monitor campaign performance to ensure that objectives are met and ROI is achieved.

As the digital landscape continues to evolve, influencer marketing is likely to remain a valuable tool for businesses looking to connect with their audience in a more authentic and engaging way. By harnessing the power of influencers, businesses can amplify their message, expand their reach, and drive meaningful connections with their target audience in the competitive digital marketplace.

CONCLUSION

Navigating the Digital Landscape

In the ever-evolving digital landscape, mastering marketing strategies is essential for businesses to thrive and stay ahead of the competition. Throughout this book, we've explored various facets of digital marketing, from understanding consumer behaviour to leveraging advanced tactics for reaching and engaging target audiences.

We began by delving into the fundamentals of marketing, emphasizing the importance of understanding consumer needs, preferences, and motivations. We then explored the power of storytelling and content marketing, highlighting how compelling narratives and valuable content can capture audience attention and foster meaningful connections with customers.

Moving forward, we explored the realm of social media marketing, discussing strategies for building communities, creating engaging content, and leveraging social advertising to reach and engage target audiences effectively. We also delved into the realms of email marketing, search engine optimization (SEO), pay-per-click (PPC) advertising, conversion rate optimization (CRO), and reputation management, exploring tactics and best practices for maximizing results in each area.

As we conclude this journey, it's clear that successful digital marketing requires a combination of creativity, data-driven insights, and continuous optimization. By understanding consumer behaviour, crafting compelling content, leveraging digital channels effectively, and measuring performance, businesses can achieve their marketing objectives and drive growth in the competitive digital landscape.

In today's digital age, adaptability and innovation are key. As technologies evolve and consumer preferences shift, businesses must remain agile and proactive in their approach to marketing. By staying informed about emerging trends, experimenting with new tactics, and embracing a culture of learning and adaptation, businesses can stay ahead of the curve and position themselves for long-term success.

As you apply the insights and strategies outlined in this book to your own marketing efforts, remember that success is a journey, not a destination. Continuously evaluate and refine your strategies, listen to your audience, and stay true to your brand's values and objectives. With dedication, creativity, and perseverance, you can navigate the digital landscape with confidence and achieve your marketing goals.

Thank you for joining us on this journey through the world of digital marketing. Here's to your success in the dynamic and ever-changing digital landscape!

www.ingramcontent.com/pod-product-compliance
Lightning Source LLC
Chambersburg PA
CBHW050458290526
45786CB00006B/2340